21st CENTURY LIVES
REALITY TV STARS

Adam Sutherland

WAYLAND

First published in 2009 by Wayland

Copyright © Wayland 2009

Wayland
338 Euston Road
London NW1 3BH

Wayland Australia
Level 17/207 Kent Street
Sydney, NSW 2000

Senior editor: Camilla Lloyd
Designer: Simon Borrough
Picture researcher: Diana Morris

Picture Acknowledgments: The author and publisher would like to thank the following for allowing their pictures to be reproduced in this publication: Cover & 10: David M Bennett/Getty Images; Chris Ratcliffe/Rex Features: 19, David Fisher/Rex Features: 18, Gregory Pace/Rex Features: 6, ITV/Rex Features: 17, 20, James Curley/Rex Features: 4, Jo Hale/Getty Images: 11, Jonathan Hordie/ Rex Features: 8, 16, Ken McKay/Rex Features: 7, Ray Tang/Rex Features: 9, Rex Features: 1, 5, 13, 14, 15, Show Biz Ireland/Getty Images: 21, Sipa/Rex Features: 12.

British Library Cataloguing in Publication Data:
Sutherland, Adam
    Reality TV stars. - (21st century lives)
    1. Reality television programs - Juvenile literature
    2. Television personalities - Biography - Juvenile
    literature
    I. Title
    791.4'5'028'0922

ISBN: 978 0 7502 5690 2

Printed in China

Wayland is a division of Hachette Children's Books, an Hachette UK company

www.hachette.co.uk

Contents

Jordan
A One-Woman Business Empire

Katie signing copies of her third autobiography, Pushed To The Limit.

"I love [being a role model]. I've come from nothing, and I've made something of myself, and I don't stop. You do have to tell people to be realistic. But I don't think there is anything that I've wanted to do that hasn't happened yet."

To Fay Weldon, *The Sunday Times*,
17 February 2008

Name: Katrina Amy Alexandria Alexis Infield, also known as Katie Price

Date and place of birth: 22 May 1978 in Brighton, East Sussex, England

Big break: Katie had been a popular glamour model for several years, but her rise to national prominence, and the start of 'her empire', came with her appearance on ITV1's *I'm A Celebrity... Get Me Out Of Here!* in 2004, and her resulting romance with fellow contestant, singer Peter Andre.

Subsequent TV appearances: From the time Katie and Peter left the jungle, their lives have been one long TV show. Programmes have included *Jordan: Living With A Dream, When Jordan Met Peter, Jordan And Peter: Laid Bare*, and the *Katie and Peter* series of shows for ITV2 that have also been broadcast on E! Channel in the USA, helping to boost Katie's popularity in America.

All-round achievements: Katie released *Being Jordan*, the first of her autobiographies, in May 2004. Turned down by all the major book companies, she signed with a small independent publisher, did a ten-day nationwide book signing tour, and shot to Number 1 in the hardback sales charts. *Being Jordan* had sold more than one million copies as of January 2007. Two further autobiographies followed, *Jordan: A Whole New World* in April 2006, and *Pushed To The Limit* in February 2008. Her first ghostwritten novel *Angel* (ghostwritten means that an author wrote the book on Jordan's behalf) was released in June 2006 and sold 300,000 copies in the first six weeks.

Something you might not know about her: Katie once stood as a candidate in the 2001 General Election in the borough of Stretford and Urmston.

Model, author, mother, TV star and incredibly successful businesswoman, Katie Price turned her 2004 appearance on ITV1's *I'm A Celebrity... Get Me Out Of Here!* into her first step on the road to national and international fame and fortune. She is now seen as a role model and she is the face of a successful brand. Millions of girls aspire to be like her.

When Katie entered the jungle she was a glamour model nearing the end of her career. While she was there she met and fell in love with Australian singer Peter Andre and the rest, as they say, is history.

The couple's entertaining and loving antics have been exhaustively documented across a series of TV documentaries from 2004 to the present day, covering every aspect of their personal lives from *Jordan: Model Mum* for BBC Choice, to *When Jordan Met Peter* for ITV and *Katie & Peter: The Baby Diaries* for ITV2.

Katie is the mother of three children, Harvey (born 27 May 2002) – from a previous relationship – is autistic and partially-sighted. Katie and Peter also have two children together, Junior Savva Andreas Andre, born on 13 June 2005, and Katie's first daughter Princess Tiáamii Crystal Esther Andre, born 29 June 2007. Most unexpected has been Katie's huge success as an author. Working with a regular ghostwriter, she has produced three autobiographies, selling more than one million hardbacks, and has more recently embarked on a series of novels about young girls fighting to succeed as models (*Angel*) and singers (*Crystal*). The novels have already sold more than half a million copies, and one of her series of children's books, *My Pony Care Book*, was nominated for WH Smith's Children's Book of the Year.

Katie is currently estimated to be worth over £30 million, and she remains as hard-working, down to earth and ambitious as ever.

> "While many celebrities lose their dignity in the jungle, she found hers. She came across as vulnerable, funny, needy and very human."
>
> Simon Hatterstone, *The Guardian,* 22 March 2008

Leona Lewis
The Bright Shining Reality Star

Leona, seen here attending the MTV Awards show in New York, is the first X Factor star to break America.

"I can't ever imagine wanting to distance myself from *The X Factor*, or having a bad word to say about it, because the show opened doors for me that had never opened before."

To journalist Chrissy Iley, 2008

Name: Leona Louise Lewis

Date and place of birth: 3 April 1985 in Stoke Newington, Hackney, east London to a Guyanese father and a Welsh mother

Education: From the age of five, Leona attended the prestigious Sylvia Young Theatre School. At nine, she moved to the Italia Conti Academy, and at 14 she studied at London's number one performing arts college The BRIT School, where Amy Winehouse was a former pupil.

Big break: In December 2006, Leona won ITV1's *The X Factor*, and a £1 million record contract. Her first single, a cover of Kelly Clarkson's *A Moment Like This,* broke world records when it was downloaded 50,000 times in the first 30 minutes of release. The single also made the 2006 Christmas Number 1, outselling the rest of the UK Top 40's sales combined. It was the most successful launch of any TV talent show contestant ever.

Subsequent TV appearances: Leona took America by storm following her performance of *Bleeding Love* on the influential Oprah Winfrey show in early 2008. She became the first British woman to top the US pop chart since Kim Wilde 20 years earlier.

All-round achievements: Simon Cowell, Leona's mentor on *The X Factor* series, negotiated a £5 million, five-album deal in the US with the legendary music executive Clive Davis, who discovered Whitney Houston. Leona's list of awards and nominations is exhaustive – Brit Award and Ivor Novello Award for *A Moment Like This,* Brit nominations for British Breakthrough Act, British Female Solo Artist, British Single and British Album.

Something you might not know about her: Leona is close friends with singer Katie Melua. The pair were classmates at The BRIT School.

Leona Lewis has arguably the greatest voice and the brightest future of any British musical reality show winner so far.

Big on talent, but initially lacking in confidence, the shy Leona battled loneliness and homesickness to astound *The X Factor* judges and viewers with her assured performances week after week. She grew in confidence over the course of the series, transforming from a pretty 21 year old into a stunning diva, beating the more assured 18 year old Ray Quinn in a final watched by 13 million viewers.

The exotically beautiful but down-to-earth girl from Hackney, east London is *The X Factor's* greatest ever find, and is already a huge success on both sides of the Atlantic.

Leona's debut album *Spirit* sold one million copies in the UK in its first five weeks on sale, making it the fastest-selling debut album ever. It debuted at Number 1 in the US Billboard 200 chart, and earned four Brit Award nominations. The single *Bleeding Love* was the UK's best-selling single of 2007, topped 30 national charts, including France, Germany, Australia and the USA where it was Number 1 for four weeks.

Although undoubtedly Leona had the talent to succeed without the huge profile boost she received from *The X Factor*, she had laboured in jobs with few prospects after leaving school and invested all her money in studio time to record several overlooked demos.

Now she's working with the world's most successful producers and songwriters, including Dallas Austin (who has worked with Madonna and Pink), Akon (who has produced for Gwen Stefani), Ne-Yo (who has written for Rihanna and Beyonce) and JR Rotem (who writes for Britney Spears).

Despite being praised as the bright shining star the music industry needs, Leona tries to keep her feet on the ground, still living in her old two-bedroom flat in Hackney, and in close contact with her close-knit family and friends. She is a woman who loves to sing. And the world loves to hear her.

According to Simon Cowell, Leona is "one of the best singers we've seen in this country for a long, long time."

"I was knocked out by her range, her versatility and the pure beauty of her voice. She is an artist who will be a true star for many years to come."

Clive Davis, 2008

Ben Fogle

Real-life Action Man

Ben regularly writes about his travels for the Daily Telegraph and The Independent, and has written three books about his adventures.

> "When I was crossing the Atlantic with [Olympic rower] James Cracknell, I nearly died when I was thrown overboard by a freak wave. Luckily another wave threw me back towards the boat."
>
> Interview with Cassandra Jardine, *The Telegraph*, January 2008

Name: Ben Fogle

Date and place of birth: 3 November 1973 in Dorset, England

Education: Ben was a pupil at Bryanston School in Dorset. He then went to the University of Portsmouth to read Latin American Studies, which included a placement at the University of Costa Rica. His globe-trotting days had begun.

Big break: In 2000 Ben volunteered to be marooned on Taransay, a remote windswept island in the Outer Hebrides as part of the BBC1 reality show *Castaway 2000*. The programme followed a group of 36 people marooned for a year starting on 1 January 2000. The castaways, including eight children, lived in modern 'mud huts', built their own school, and reared their own cattle, sheep, pigs and chickens. The series was a huge success, with viewing figures of nearly nine million.

Subsequent TV appearances: The viewers loved Ben, and so did the BBC. Since leaving Taransay, he has presented a wide range of different programmes for the channel, including *Animal Park, Countryfile, Wild in Africa, Crufts, One Man and His Dog, Holiday*, and most recently the new adventure series, *Extreme Dreams* in 2008.

All-round achievements: Ben won a Royal Television Society (RTS) award for the highly acclaimed *Through Hell and High Water* – a show following his Atlantic crossing with Olympic Gold medallist rower James Cracknell – and has been nominated as TV personality of the year and as best new talent. His first book, *The Teatime Islands*, was short-listed for the WH Smith's People's Award for Best Travel Book.

Something you might not know about him: Ben was trained by Frank Bruno for a three-round charity boxing match against *EastEnders* actor Sid Owen for BBC Sport Relief. Ben won!

TV presenter, writer and all-round action man, Ben Fogle showed an interest in both travel and broadcasting from an early age. He spent his gap year before university working in an orphanage in Ecuador. And then a further four years were spent in South America following his degree, including a spell at a turtle conservation project on the Mosquito Coast of Honduras.

Back in England, Ben quickly got itchy feet, and left the security of a job at society magazine *Tatler* to throw himself into the BBC's 'millennium project' – the hugely successful reality TV show *Castaway 2000*.

The island's golden boy – charming, level-headed and infinitely practical – Ben quickly found himself a niche on the channel's more 'cuddly' output from *Crufts* to *Countryfile*, where he has reported on the UK's weird and wonderful rural pastimes, including worm charming, lawn mower racing, cheese rolling and Morris dancing. In 2008 Ben took part in the World Coal Carrying Championships in Gawthorpe, West Yorkshire and finished in a respectable 22nd place.

Ben has always had a taste for adventure, and has notched up some amazing – and death-defying – exploits over the years. He has completed the Marathon Des Sables, a 160-mile, six-day race across the Sahara desert, and more recently rowed across the Atlantic Ocean with Double Olympic gold medal-winning oarsman, James Cracknell. The pair did the crossing in 49 days, setting a new British record. The BBC series that followed them, *Through Hell and High Water*, won a Royal Television Society award in 2007.

In 2008 Ben teamed up with James Cracknell once again to take part in a race to the South Pole, the first

Ben, and Olympic rower James Cracknell, help launch a rowing race for BBC Children in Need.

in 97 years, since the great Norwegian-British race between Roald Amundsen and Robert Falcon Scott. The route covered nearly 370 miles and took two months to complete, across one of the least hospitable environments on earth. The team competed for Great Britain against an international line up of teams including New Zealand, Norway, Italy, Russia and the USA. The race is due to be aired on TV in 2009.

"Ben Fogle seems unable to resist a challenge, however terrifying or unpleasant. As long as there is a humid, bug-infested jungle to explore, or an ice floe on which to battle against gale force winds, he'll be there."

Cassandra Jardine, *The Telegraph*, January 2008

Cheryl Cole
Girl Band Superstar

Cheryl arriving at the 2008 Brit Awards. Her band Girls Aloud, were nominated for Best British Group.

"I can hardly believe it. Four months ago I was sitting in a council house drinking tea and watching Oprah Winfrey on television all day. "

Cheryl, shortly after winning the greatest number of viewer votes to secure a place in the band in 2002

Name: Cheryl Ann Cole (born Cheryl Ann Tweedy)

Date and place of birth: 30 June 1983 in Heaton, Newcastle upon Tyne, England

Education: School came second to Cheryl's ambitions to perform. She began modelling at the age of three, appeared in a British Gas advert aged seven and joined the Royal Ballet's summer school two years later. By the time Cheryl was 12 she had decided to pursue a singing career, signing with a management company and attending countless auditions.

Big break: Cheryl was working as a waitress when she decided to take part in ITV1's reality show *Popstars: The Rivals* in 2002, a competition to find a girl group and a boy band simultaneously. Cheryl was the first member of the girl band to be selected by voters, and with fellow contestants Sarah Harding, Nadine Coyle, Nicola Roberts and Kimberley Walsh became Girls Aloud.

Subsequent TV appearances: Cheryl presented her own TV show for ITV2 as part of the *Passions of Girls Aloud* series, where she went to Los Angeles to audition as a breakdancer for a will-i-am music video. Most recently, Cheryl has been one of the judges on *The X Factor* on ITV1.

All-round achievements: Before she joined Girls Aloud, Cheryl was a successful child model, and won several beauty contests including Boots Bonniest Baby, Mothercare Happy Faces Portrait contest, and Best Looking Girl in Newcastle.

Something you might not know about her: Cheryl has two entries in the Guinness Book of Records, with Girls Aloud – 'Most Successful Reality TV Group' in the 2007 edition, and 'Most Consecutive Top Ten Entries in the UK by a Female Group' in the 2008 edition.

Cheryl and her Girls Aloud bandmates, from left to right, Nadine Coyle, Cheryl, Nicola Roberts, Sarah Harding and Kimberley Walsh.

Like all the best overnight successes, it actually took Cheryl Cole years to become a star. From bonny baby beauty contests, to dancing and singing at shopping centres across the north east, she showed the dedication and hard work required to make it to the top.

Even so, no one would have been surprised to see manufactured pop band Girls Aloud – Cheryl along with Nadine Coyle, Nicola Roberts, Sarah Harding and Kimberley Walsh – fizzle out after a couple of albums. Instead, the girls have become one of the most successful British pop groups of all time, with a record-breaking 18 consecutive Top 10 singles (including three Number 1s) and five platinum albums. They are Smash Hits poll winners, have won a TMF Award and have been nominated for two Brit Awards.

The band hold the record for the shortest time between formation and reaching Number 1 in the UK Charts (with their platinum-selling debut single *Sound Of The Underground*), and have become one of the few reality TV groups to achieve continued success.

Backed by the ground-breaking British production team Xenomania, the girls' music ranges from the distinctly 1980s' sound of *No Good Advice* and *Jump* through the 1960s' sound of *Love Machine* to the more futuristic sound of *The Show, Sexy! No No No...* and *The Promise*.

The Guinness Book of Records lists them as 'Most Successful Reality TV Group' in the 2007 edition, and they also hold the record for 'Most Consecutive Top Ten Entries in the UK by a Female Group' in the 2008 edition, with 15 consecutive top 10s from *Sound of the Underground* in 2002 through to *Walk This Way* in 2007. Girls Aloud have since extended this record to 18 consecutive Top 10s from debut — the most recent being *The Promise*, which reached Number 2 in November 2008. Girls Aloud have sold 2.2m albums, including 850,000 copies of 2007's *Greatest Hits*.

In July 2006, Cheryl signed a deal worth a reported £200,000 to become the face of Coca Cola Zero for its UK launch. The same year, she got married to Chelsea and England footballer Ashley Cole at the five-star Sopwell House Hotel near St Albans. The couple also held a £500, 000 wedding party at Wrotham Park in Hertfordshire, sponsored by *OK! Magazine*. Even so, Cheryl manages to remain charming, down-to-earth, and as hard-working as ever.

"As much as anything, [Cheryl's] mix of the magnetically glamorous and the naturally down-to-earth might be the best explanation of [her] universal appeal."

Jon Wilde, *The Daily Mail*, 2 September 2007

Kelly Osbourne
The Eternal Teenage Tearaway

Fashion-conscious Kelly counts Kate Moss and Lily Allen among her friends.

"My personal life is made public to the world ... but, you know what, as far as I'm concerned I sold my soul to the devil. I wanted to be famous. I wanted to do the TV shows, so you take the bad with the good."

To journalist Ian Burrell in *The Independent*, 9 June 2008

Name: Kelly Michelle Lee Osbourne

Date and place of birth: 27 October 1984 in London, England

Education: Kelly grew up on the road, living in more than 20 different homes as she toured the world with her father, veteran heavy metal singer Ozzy Osbourne, and his band. From the age of 12, Kelly and the family moved to Los Angeles where she lived until she graduated from high school.

Big break: *The Osbournes*, a crazy, foul-mouthed, award-winning MTV reality show featured the daily lives of Kelly, her brother Jack, and mum and dad, Ozzy and Sharon. The show broadcast around the world, and ran for four series and 52 episodes, from 2002 to 2005.

Subsequent TV appearances: Kelly has presented the *MTV Movie Awards* (2002), MTV UK and Ireland's red carpet coverage of the 2003 *MTV Europe Music Awards, Top of the Pops Saturday* on BBC2, and *Popworld* and *The Friday Night Project* on Channel 4. In January 2007, Kelly began presenting *Project Catwalk* for Sky One, taking over from previous presenter, Liz Hurley. In autumn 2007, she joined BBC Radio 1 to host the Sunday night teen show, *Radio 1's Surgery*.

All-round achievements: Kelly had a UK Number 1 single in 2003 with *Changes*, a duet with dad Ozzy. In the theatre, she has played the role of Mama Morton in London's long-running hit musical *Chicago*, and won Glamour Magazine's Theatre Actress of the Year Award for her performance.

Something you might not know about her: Kelly has her brother Jack's name tattooed on her wrist, and a tattoo of a padlock and key with the word 'Daddy'.

With her bright red lips, shock of (usually) black hair, tattoos, and razor sharp tongue, Kelly Osbourne has gone from stroppy 15-year-old in worldwide TV sensation *The Osbournes*, to chart-topping recording artist, talented TV presenter and award-winning stage actress. Not bad for the girl who admits she spent most of her teenage years on the sofa watching TV and feared she would turn out to be 'the biggest loser'.

Kelly, with mum and dad Sharon and Ozzy, who co-presented the 2008 Brit Awards.

Kelly's big break came with the runaway hit reality series *The Osbournes* for MTV, chronicling the day-to-day lives of a dysfunctional, but truly loving family. The show premiered on 5 March 2002, and in its first season was cited as the most-viewed series ever on MTV. The final episode of the final season aired 21 March 2005.

Riding the wave of the show's success, Kelly initially followed her dad into music. Her debut album *Shut Up!* was released in 2002 by Epic Records, and included a cover version of Madonna's song *Papa Don't Preach*. Changing record labels the following year to Sanctuary, she released *Changes*, which produced her first UK Number 1 hit single, and in 2005 she released *Sleeping In the Nothing*.

Since then, Kelly has put music on the back burner, and has found success both as a TV presenter - where she has worked regularly for MTV at awards ceremonies, and has co-hosted ITV2's *I'm A Celebrity... Get Me Out Of Here!* coverage - and as a stage actress, winning the Glamour Magazine Theatre Actress of the Year Award for her role as Mama Morton in London's West End production of *Chicago*.

A friend of Kate Moss, Amy Winehouse, and Lily Allen, Kelly is also well-known for her sharp fashion sense, winning style awards from Elle magazine and LK Today.

From 2004 to 2006, she ran her own fashion line, Stiletto Killers, producing a range of T-shirts, hoodies and sweatpants featuring cartoon designs and punk rock phrases and, more recently, she was the face of High Street chain Accessorize, for an advertising campaign that ran across Europe, South America, Asia and the Middle East.

Kelly is currently teen agony columnist for *The Sun* newspaper, and a successful radio DJ with her show *Radio 1's Surgery* broadcasting every Sunday evening from 10pm–midnight. With a childhood like Kelly's, we can't think of a better agony aunt.

"A wickedly funny, brutally honest, pint-size, potty-mouthed spitfire …"

Journalist Jenny Eliscu writing in the December 2002 issue of *Rolling Stone* for her feature 'Kelly Osbourne'

Will Young
The Smooth Operator

After winning Pop Idol, *Will has grown into a successful and well-respected international singing star.*

Name: William Robert Young

Date and place of birth: 20 January 1979 in Wokingham, Berkshire, England

Education: Will attended Hollis Hill prep school and Wellington College, before moving on to D'Overbroeck's College, Oxford, and then studying politics at the University of Exeter. In September 2001, he began a three-year course in musical theatre at the Arts Educational School in Chiswick, London.

Big break: In February 2002, Will won the first series of *Pop Idol* on ITV1, beating the widely tipped frontrunner Gareth Gates who won second place. Although Will was generally seen as the underdog throughout the series, it later emerged that he topped the voting in six out of the nine rounds of public voting. Will's first single, a cover of Westlife's *Evergreen*, sold 400,000 copies on the first day of release, and over 1.7 million copies in total.

Subsequent TV appearances: Will found himself back on the big screen in 2005, this time as an actor, starring alongside Dame Judi Dench and Bob Hoskins in the BBC film *Mrs Henderson Presents*. He has also presented documentaries for BBC Children In Need.

All-round achievements: Will has been nominated for eight Brit Awards and won two, as Best Breakthrough Act in 2003, and for the single *Your Game* in 2005. He was also voted the UK's favourite artist of all time in 2006 and 2007 by commercial radio listeners.

Something you might not know about him: Will has a non-identical twin brother called Rupert, who runs a non-profit organisation called The Mood Foundation.

"I've had three premonitions in my life. One of them was *Pop Idol*. Very specific feelings. I just knew I'd win a show. I knew there would be a show that would look for one person and if that show came along it would be perfect for me and I'd probably win it. Weird."

Interview with Sylvia Patterson for *The Telegraph*, August 2008

Will Young is the charming, well-spoken 'boy-next-door' who won the debut series of ITV1's *Pop Idol* in 2002, beating 'the nation's favourite' Gareth Gates, and went on to achieve lasting commercial and critical success as a singer, performer and songwriter.

Will had left university and won a scholarship to musical theatre college when *Pop Idol* came along. Will's confident, mature performances of 1960s' soul classics from the likes of The Drifters, Aretha Franklin and Bill Withers brought him through the show as the hands-down winner.

Will's first double A-side single *Evergreen/ Anything Is Possible* became the fastest-selling debut in chart history, selling over 400,000 copies on the day of release, 1.7 million copies overall, and winning an Ivor Novello Award for Best Song Musically and Lyrically.

More chart and critical success followed, with a Brit Award in 2003 for Best Breakthrough Act in recognition of his debut album *From Now On*, and a second Brit for the single *Your Game* in 2005.

In his work as well as his live performances Will likes to break new boundaries. He performed *We Are The Champions* with Queen members Brian May and Roger Taylor at Buckingham Palace for the Queen's Jubilee Concert in 2002. He also sung with soul legend James Brown on tour in 2004, and with the Vanguard Big Band at historic Ronnie Scott's Jazz Club in 2007 and 2008. He has also performed at Glastonbury and T in the Park (where he danced the Highland Fling), and at the Olympics hand-over party in London.

Will's best-known singles - *Leave Right Now, Friday's Child, Switch It On, Who Am I* and *Changes* are some of the finest of the decade, further enhanced by their comic videos, where Will often shows that he doesn't take his fame and celebrity status too seriously.

With his fourth album, *Let It Go*, released in September 2008, and a 20-date UK tour already booked and sold out, Will Young is still as hard-working and successful as ever.

Will performs at the Pop Idol *concert at Wembley in 2002.*

"Will Young seems less like a star with diva pretentions, and more like a good mate, someone who's fun to have around and easy to talk to."

Michael Hubbard, 2005, http://www.musicomh.com/interviews/will-young_1105.htm

Myleene Klass
The Most Famous Girl-next-door

Name: Myleene Klass

Date and place of birth: 6 April 1978 in Gorleston, Norfolk, England to an Austrian-English father and a Filipina mother

Education: Myleene attended Notre Dame High School in Norwich, but spent her Saturdays studying singing at the junior department of the Guildhall School of Music and Drama in London, and later won a scholarship to the prestigious musical theatre course at the Royal Academy of Music at the University of London.

Big break: Myleene's big break was on *Popstars*, ITV1's first musical reality series in 2001. From thousands of hopefuls, Myleene was chosen to become one of five members of the UK's first reality pop band, Hear'Say. The band's first single *Pure and Simple* entered the charts at number 1, going on to sell more than one million copies.

Subsequent TV appearances: In 2006, Myleene spent three weeks in the Australian jungle as part of ITV1's massive reality show *I'm A Celebrity... Get Me Out Of Here!* After only one week on the show, she became the most searched for celebrity from the show ever on Internet search engine MSN, and the third most searched for celebrity overall in the world. By the last week of the show, Myleene became the most searched for celebrity in the world by UK users.

All-round achievements: Myleene began playing the piano and her grandfather's violin at the age of four. In 2003, she signed a five-album deal with Universal Classics and released her first solo classical album *Moving On*. Entering the classical charts at number 2, the album went on to break sales records.

Something you might not know about her: Myleene comes from six generations of classical musicians on her father's side. Her grandmother was an opera singer.

A trained pianist, violinist and singer, Myleene has topped both the pop and the classical charts.

> **"I love the opportunities that [reality shows] create for people that would otherwise be overlooked. For everyone who comes dressed as a banana singing 'I Am What I Am', there's a Leona Lewis."**
>
> **The Observer, Sunday 27 July 2008**

Singer, musician, TV presenter, reality show star, and now model, Myleene Klass first became famous as one of the five members of Hear'Say. The band were the first reality stars on the first series of ITV1's *Popstars* in 2001 – the forerunner to both *Pop Idol* and *The X Factor* – and achieved incredible success.

Their first single *Pure And Simple* was the fastest-selling non-charitable record ever, selling 1.3 million copies, their debut album *Popstars* sold 1.2 million copies, and they sold out a 37-date UK arena tour. But what goes up, must come down, and less than a year after they formed, the band had split up and gone their separate ways.

Anyone who thought that would be the last they heard of Myleene, though, would be proved very wrong. The classically trained pianist quickly bounced back with a five-album deal with Universal Classics and another record-breaking debut album *Moving On*.

By 2005, Myleene was turning her attentions back to television, and for six months presented the hit ITV1 Saturday morning music show *CD:UK*. Her presenting work ranged from the BBC's coverage of *The Proms* to *Ghost Town* for Living TV and *The All Star Talent Show* for Channel Five.

What pushed Myleene's profile into the UK's A-list, however, was her appearance on ITV1's *I'm A Celebrity... Get Me Out Of Here!* She finished second to ex-boy band star Matt Willis, but walked away a winner in TV and commercial terms, accepting offers to present *The People's Quiz* and *The One* for BBC1, launching her own movie show, *The Screening Room*, on CNN International, and signing with Marks and Spencer to be the face of their 2007 and 2008 advertising campaigns alongside supermodel Erin O'Connor and 1960s' icon Twiggy.

Myleene with fellow I'm A Celebrity ... contestants Matt Willis (left, the eventual winner) and Jason Donovan (right).

Even the birth of her first baby, Ava, in 2007 didn't slow Myleene down. She wrote about her pregnancy in a best-selling diary *My Bump And Me*, and even launched a range of baby clothes, Baby K, in association with Mothercare. With her hard work, dedication, and undoubted talent, Myleene has earned every minute of her success.

"It is almost impossible not to like Myleene or admire the tenacious way in which she has pursued the goals she set for herself all those years ago. A lot of hard work has gone into getting here."

Jane Gordon, 24 March 2007, http://www.dailymail.co.uk/you/article-444227/Why-Myleene-Klass-unhappy-size-8.html

Lee Mead
The Leading Man

Lee's performances as Joseph have been described as 'faultless', 'charismatic' and 'perfect'.

66 **Some people think I went on the programme for the fame. If this [role] had come through a normal way, I would have auditioned for it normally. I was there for the role and nothing else. I would have walked away with my head high whether I'd won or lost.** 99

Interview with Jasper Rees in *The Telegraph*, 11 July 2007

Name: Lee Stephen Mead

Date and place of birth: 14 July 1981, in Southend-on-Sea, Essex, England

Big break: Lee is best known as the winner of the BBC1 reality talent show *Any Dream Will Do* in June 2007. The show saw 12 contestants compete for the lead role in a West End revival of *Joseph And The Amazing Technicolor Dreamcoat* under the watchful eye of the show's composer and co-producer, Andrew Lloyd Webber. Lee, who had previously spent time as an understudy on the show for a regional tour, was chosen by the judges in the final show and was widely praised for his confidence, showmanship and stage presence. As the show's winner, Lee initially gained a six-month contract to appear in *Joseph*, but such were the show's advance bookings, and the critical reaction to his performances, that his contract was quickly extended, first to June 2008, and then on to January 2009.

Subsequent TV appearances: In his first public performance after winning the role, Lee sang *Any Dream Will Do* in front of 60,000 people at Wembley Stadium and a TV audience of two billion, alongside former Josephs Donny Osmond and Jason Donovan for Prince William and Prince Harry's Concert for Diana.

All-round achievements: Lee has also released a double A-side single *Any Dream Will Do/Close Every Door* with fellow finalists Lewis Bradley and Keith Jack to raise money for BBC's Children In Need. His album *Lee Mead,* including a song written for him by Take That's Gary Barlow, has sold over 200,000 copies.

Something you might not know about him: Lee was crowned Rear of the Year in September 2007, alongside female winner Sian Lloyd!

Lee Mead is the understudy that became a leading man. He was one of 12 contestants on BBC1's primetime Saturday night search to find a new Joseph for Andrew Lloyd Webber's production of his award-winning stage show in 2007. Lee battled it out to prove that he was talented enough to get people into the theatre seats, and to follow in the footsteps of charismatic stage Josephs before him, including Phillip Schofield and Jason Donovan.

Lee's performances throughout the series were always of the highest quality. However, there was occasional criticism aimed at him because he was already seen as 'the professional', having previously featured in a touring production of Joseph for a year, directed and produced by the *Any Dream Will Do* panel judge Bill Kenwright. What's more, to be able to compete in the show Lee had to break his contract with a production of Andrew Lloyd Webber's *Phantom of the Opera*.

But there's no denying that Lee worked hard to get his big break. His first leading role was as a 15-year-old Danny in the school production of *Grease*. He was bitten by the performing bug, and left musical theatre college early to take up a job as an entertainer on ferries to and from the Bay of Biscay, performing on dancefloors covered in broken glass, and dodging abuse from drunken passengers. His next booking was a summer season at the 1,500-seater Bridlington Spa Theatre, where Lee regularly played to audiences of 35, and once sang his final song to the barking of a dog in the theatre!

Lee has proved a huge success as Joseph. Before opening night, the producers had taken over £10 million in ticket sales.

Now Lee has made a critical and commercial success of his role in Joseph, had a chart-topping album *Lee Mead*, has a celebrity girlfriend (*Any Dream Will Do* panel judge Denise van Outen) and a career on the West End stage. His success proves that hard work can pay off.

Lee looks set to be in the spotlight for many years to come.

"Unusually among reality TV contestants, [Lee] is a trained actor who worked his way up the hard way via cruise ships, summer stock and understudying."

Nick Curtis, *Evening Standard*, 20 July 2007

Kerry Katona
The People's Favourite

Name: Kerry Jayne Elizabeth Katona

Date and place of birth: 6 September 1980, in Warrington, Cheshire, England

Big break: In February 2004, Kerry won the third series of *I'm A Celebrity... Get Me Out Of Here!* watched by a record 15 million viewers. The public took Kerry and her down-to-earth nature to their hearts and she has been a permanent feature on TV and in gossip magazines ever since.

Subsequent TV appearances: Kerry and her husband Mark Croft also had their own 'Jordan and Peter-style' 12-part documentary series *Kerry Katona: Crazy In Love* on MTV in early 2008. The series ended prematurely when Kerry went into hospital to give birth to her fourth child, son Maxwell, in April 2008.

All-round achievements: Kerry was one of the founding members of Liverpool girl group Atomic Kitten, which she joined when she was 16. The band released six singles and an album *Right Now* in March 2000, and had a UK Number 1 single with *Whole Again* in 2001. Kerry left the band shortly afterwards, when she became pregnant with her first child, Molly, to Westlife singer Brian McFadden.

Something you might not know about her: Kerry sang on Atomic Kitten's first Number 1 single *Whole Again*, but left the band before it reached the top of the charts. The single was re-recorded with Jenny Frost, Kerry's replacement band member.

Despite a troubled childhood, Kerry has achieved success as a singer, a writer and a TV personality.

"I thought it was a great interview [with Jonathan Ross]. He gave me the chance to speak for myself. That's all I ask for – honesty. That's why I am doing an MTV documentary to show the real me."

Inteview with Rachael Bletchly, www.people.co.uk, 2008

Kerry at a book signing of her autobiography *Too Much, Too Young*.

Kerry Katona overcame a childhood of neglect, domestic violence and periods in foster homes to form one-third of Atomic Kitten, one of Britain's most popular and successful girl groups of the last ten years.

Kerry left the band in 2001 after the band enjoyed their first UK Number 1 single *Whole Again* when she discovered she was pregnant to then-boyfriend, the Westlife singer Brian McFadden. The pair married in January 2002 and have two daughters together, Molly and Lilly-Sue, but sadly separated in 2004, six months after Kerry was crowned Queen of the Jungle in ITV1's third series of *I'm A Celebrity*...

Kerry started her jungle adventure scared of her own shadow, but she rolled up her sleeves, confronted her fears head on, and emerged a hugely entertaining and popular winner in a show watched by an all-time high of 15 million viewers. She even did better than Katie Price (also known as Jordan) in a Bush Tucker Trial face-off, when the pair had to eat mealworms, cockroaches, green ants, witchety grubs and fish eyes. They matched each other snack for snack until Jordan fell at the last hurdle, spitting out her fish eye when it burst on her tongue. The pair's Trial was named in viewers' Top 10 favourites of all-time recently.

Since the jungle, Kerry's profile has grown hugely, with a weekly column in celebrity magazine *OK!*, her own 12-episode reality series *Kerry Katona: Crazy In Love* on MTV, and advertising and endorsement work for supermarket chains Iceland and Asda.

Kerry's 2006 autobiography *Too Much Too Young: My Story Of Love, Survival And Celebrity* has sold over 400,000 copies and, like her old friend Katie Price, she has since gone on to write semi-autobiographical novels *Tough Love* and *The Footballer's Wife*.

With her tangled home life, and truly engaging personality, Kerry will continue to have her ups and downs – on camera and very definitely in the full glare of the media spotlight. But let's hope that she continues to be successful, and to remain happy and settled.

> "I can stay in my house for a month and not go out, yet I guarantee I'll still be on the front of a magazine at least twice a week."
>
> Kerry to Philip Schofield and Fern Britten on 9 January 2008, on *This Morning*

Suzanne Shaw

Suzanne Shaw would be the first to admit that her career has had its share of ups and downs. At 20 years old she won *Popstars*, ITV1's first ever musical reality show, had Britain's fastest-selling record ever for the single *Pure And Simple*, and her group Hear'say had their own Saturday night TV show *Hear'say It's Saturday*.

The band toured throughout 2001, and in November of that year released their second album *Everybody*. The album only sold one-fifth of the amount sold of the first album, *Popstars*.

The band broke up in early 2002, but thanks to Suzanne's background in musical theatre, she landed the lead role in the West End production of Cliff Richard's *Summer Holiday*, and its subsequent UK tour.

In February 2005 she was offered the role of narrator in *Joseph and the Amazing Technicolor Dreamcoat* in the West End. A leading role in *The Rocky Horror Show* followed.

But Suzanne's real return to the spotlight came when she won ITV1's *Dancing On Ice* in 2008. Skating with a cracked rib and a chipped bone in her ankle, Suzanne won the affection and support of the 12 million TV viewers, beating the favourite, Hollyoaks actor Chris Fountain.

She has since been voted Celebrity Mum of the Year, and modelled high-profile lingerie designer Michelle Mone's new range Michelle for George at Asda. Suzanne is back and she's earned it!

Chico

One the most entertaining contestants to appear on UK reality TV, Chico (born Yousseph Slimani) made his name as the singing, dancing, larger-than-life contestant on the 2005 series of *The X Factor*. Born in South Wales to Muslim parents, Chico moved to Morocco with his father when he was two, where he spent time working as a mountain goat herder. At 13 he moved back to England, settling in Crawley, West Sussex.

After a four-year stint as a nightclub singer, Chico entered *The X Factor*, and caused controversy from the start – Simon Cowell even walking out in disgust after Louis Walsh and Sharon Osbourne voted him through to the second round.

Quickly finding his feet on the show, Chico's performances became more tongue-in-cheek, and his support grew, taking him all the way to the quarter finals of the competition that was eventually won by Shayne Ward.

On one of the episodes, Chico performed the self-written *It's Chico Time*, which eventually knocked Madonna off the top of the UK charts when it was released as his first single in March 2006.

More recently, Chico has appeared on ITV2's *CelebAir*, learning to run an airline alongside fellow famous faces, and continues to entertain TV viewers in his own unique style.

Shilpa Shetty

Shilpa Shetty (born 8 June 1975 in Tamil Nadu, India) is a prolific Indian film actress, model and in 2007 became the first Indian celebrity to appear in Channel 4's *Celebrity Big Brother*.

The star of more than 50 Hindi, Tamil, Telugu and Kannada language films, Shilpa was rumoured to have been paid close to £400,000 to appear on the show.

Following a worldwide media controversy that

publicised her as a target of racist bullying from other housemates, including former *Big Brother* contestant Jade Goody, Shilpa won the show with a record 63% of the public vote.

After leaving the *Big Brother* house in February 2007, Shilpa's UK profile kept growing. She met with then-British prime minister Tony Blair at the House of Commons, was invited to Marlborough House in London by Queen Elizabeth II, and was even offered a part in BBC1's *EastEnders*.

In August 2008, Shilpa presented *Bigg Boss*, the Indian version of *Big Brother*, with Jade Goody as one of the initial housemates.

Kate Lawler
The first-ever female winner of Channel 4's *Big Brother*, Kate (born in May 1980) won the third series in 2002.

A sensible, music-loving keep fit fan, Kate put her £70,000 *Big Brother* winnings towards buying her first house, released a best-selling boxercise fitness DVD and has presented various TV shows including the *RI:SE* breakfast show on Channel 4 and Channel Five's *Party In The Park*.

A life-long music fan, Kate then turned her attention to learning to DJ, and has since toured the world. She now presents *Drive!* on Kerrang Radio every day from 4–7pm.

Kate has made further reality TV show appearances in *Celebrity Wrestling* on ITV1 (2005) and *Love Island 2*, also on ITV1 (2006).

Brendan Cole
Brendan Cole (born 23 April 1976 in Christchurch, New Zealand) is a professional ballroom dancer who has appeared in five series of the BBC1 show *Strictly Come Dancing*.

Brendan has danced since he was six, and came to the United Kingdom when he was 19. Before he danced professionally he was a builder.

Particularly in the third and fourth series, Brendan often clashed with the judges over their scoring and comments on his performances, and as a result has sometimes been dubbed 'the bad boy of Strictly'.

In the first series of the show, Brendan danced with BBC newsreader Natasha Kaplinsky and the pair won the series and enjoyed a brief romance. He has since danced with *Casualty* actress Sarah Manners, GMTV's Fiona Phillips, *Bad Girls* actress Claire King, and radio presenter Lisa Snowdon.

In July and August of 2006 Brendan spent seven weeks on a Fijian Island for ITV1's *Love Island*, finishing second, and in January of 2007 he competed in the BBC1 reality hit *Just The Two of Us*.

Abbey Clancy
Abigail Rose Clancy (born in January 1986) rose to prominence in the second series of Living TV's *Britain's Next Top Model* in 2006. It was during the broadcasting of the show that the former girl band singer's relationship with the England and Portsmouth footballer Peter Crouch – then playing at the World Cup in Germany – came to light and received extensive media coverage.

Although Abbey lost in the final of the show to fashion model Lianne Fowler, she has gone on to have a far more prolific modelling and TV career than her rival. As well as advertising campaigns for Lynx, Euromillions and Matalan, Abbey was back on Living TV in 2007 with her own reality TV series *Abbey And Janice: Beauty And The Best*, which followed her attempts to break into the modelling scene in Los Angeles.

Abbey is a regular guest on shows like *Richard And Judy*, *Friday Night With Jonathan Ross* and GMTV, and was also in the third series of ITV1's *Hell's Kitchen* in 2007. Most recently she co-presented *The Fashion Show* on ITV2 with DJ George Lamb and model Michelle de Swarte.

Index

21st Century Lives

Contents of more books in the series:

British Olympians
978 0 7502 5946 0

Rebecca Romero
Ben Ainslie
Rebecca Adlington
Lee Pearson
Sarah Storey
Chris Hoy
Eleanor Simmonds
Tim Brabants
Christine Ohuruogu
Other British Olympians

Reality TV Stars
978 0 7502 5690 2

Jordan
Leona Lewis
Ben Fogle
Cheryl Cole
Kelly Osbourne
Will Young
Myleene Klass
Lee Mead
Kerry Katona
Other Reality TV Stars

Teen Movie Stars
978 0 7502 5691 9

Zac Efron
Lindsay Lohan
Daniel Radcliffe & Emma Watson
Scarlet Johansson
Hilary Duff
Freddie Highmore
Christina Ricci
Thomas Sangster
Kirsten Dunst
Other Teen Movie Stars

Radio DJs
978 0 7502 5688 9

Chris Evans
Chris Moyles
Christian O'Connell
Jo Whiley
John Peel
Johnny Vaughan
Nihal
Sara Cox
Zane Lowe
Other Radio DJs

Soap Stars
978 0 7502 5689 6

Ada Nicodemou
Jack P. Shepherd
Kara Tointon
Kym Valentine
Lacey Turner
Roxanne Pallett
Patsy Palmer
Scott Maslen
Samia Smith
Other Soap Stars

WAYLAND